# Homes

## Around the World

Clare Lewis

Raintree is an imprint of Capstone Global Library Limited, a company incorporated in England and Wales having its registered office at 7 Pilgrim Street, London, EC4V 6LB – Registered company number: 6695582

www.raintreepublishers.co.uk
myorders@raintreepublishers.co.uk

Text © Capstone Global Library Limited 2015
Paperback edition first published in 2015
The moral rights of the proprietor have been asserted.

Edited by Joanna Issa, Shelly Lyons, Diyan Leake and Helen Cox Cannons
Designed by Cynthia Akiyoshi
Original illustrations © Capstone Global Library Ltd 2014
Picture research by Elizabeth Alexander and Tracy Cummins
Production by Victoria Fitzgerald
Originated by Capstone Global Library Ltd
Printed and bound in China

ISBN 978 1 406 28195 8 (hardback)
18 17 16 15 14
10 9 8 7 6 5 4 3 2 1

ISBN 978 1 406 28203 0 (paperback)
19 18 17 16 15
10 9 8 7 6 5 4 3 2 1

**British Library Cataloguing in Publication Data**
A full catalogue record for this book is available from the British Library.

**Acknowledgements**
We would like to thank the following for permission to reproduce photographs: Alamy pp. 17 & 22e (both © Liquid Light), 20 & 22d (both © Images of Africa Photobank); Corbis pp. 11 (© Fadil), 15 (© Image Source), 16 & 22c (© George Steinmetz); Getty Images pp. 7 &23a (both Tim Draper/ Dorling Kindersley), 21 & 22a (both Elisabeth Pollaert Smith/ Photographer's Choice); iStockphoto p. 10 (© Abenaa); Shutterstock pp. 1 (© Pitcha Torranin), 2 (© Tanawat Pontchour), 3 (© antpkr), 4 (© JeniFoto), 5 (© Natali Glado), 6 (© leungchopan), 8 (© pgaborphotos), 12 (© Chantal de Bruijne), 14 (© Agnieszka Guzowska), 18 (© zebra0209), 19 (© VLADJ55), 23b (© Natali Glado), 24 (© S. R. Lee Photo Traveller); Shutterstock pp. 18 (© zebra0209), 19 (© VLADJ55), 23b (© Natali Glado), 24 (© S .R. Lee Photo Traveller); Superstock pp. 9 &22b (both Norbert Eisele-Hein/i/imagebroker.net), 13 (Nomad).

Cover photograph of homes in Venice, Italy, reproduced with permission of Superstock (Raga Jose Fuste/Prisma).

# Contents

# Homes everywhere

All around the world, people live in homes.

Homes give us shelter from the weather.

Some homes are in busy cities.

Some homes are in the countryside.

# What are homes made of?

Some homes are made of stone.

Some homes are made of wood.

Some homes are made of mud.

Some homes are made of grass.

# Different types of homes

Some homes are small.

Some homes are big.

Some homes are old.

Some homes are new.

Some homes are high up in trees.

Some homes are underground.

Some homes are in caves.

Some homes can move.

Homes are different all over
the world.

What is your home like?

# Map of homes around the world

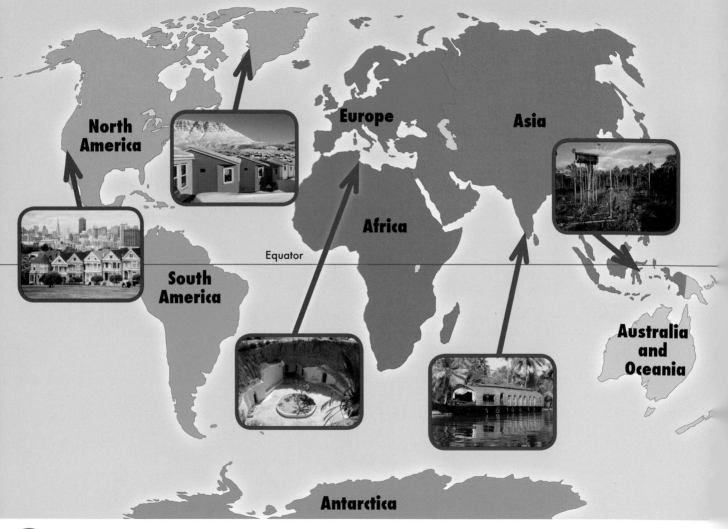

North America

Europe

Asia

Africa

South America

Equator

Australia and Oceania

Antarctica

# Picture glossary

**countryside** places that are away from towns and cities

**shelter** place to stay safe

# Index

**Notes for parents and teachers**

**Before reading**

Ask children about the types of homes they see in their community or neighbourhood (houses, blocks of flats, etc.). What types of material are these homes made of? What other materials do they think homes can be made of? Explain that, throughout the world, homes are often made from many different types of materials that are usually available from the area in which the home is built.

**After reading**

- Turn to page 5 and read the sentence. Ask children if they know what *shelter* means. Do any clues in the sentence help them know? Then turn to the glossary on page 23 and explain that a glossary is a tool that helps explain some of the more difficult words in the book. Find and read the definition for *shelter*.

- Discuss how many of the homes throughout the book are very different, but that there are some things that are similar in most homes. Have children look through the pictures and name the similar features (doors, windows, walls, roof). Have children draw a picture of their home and label these parts.